8-10

DATE DUE		
JAN 18 2011	JUN 05 2011	
FEB 04 2011		
MAR 28 2012		
APR 16 2012		

The Urbana Free Library

To renew materials call
217-367-4057

SCIENCE Q&A

CRIME

— Janice Parker —

W

Weigl Publishers Inc.

Published by Weigl Publishers Inc.
350 5th Avenue, Suite 3304, PMB 6G
New York, NY 10118-0069

Website: www.weigl.com

Library of Congress Cataloging-in-Publication Data

Parker, Janice.
  Crime / Janice Parker.
      p. cm. -- (Science Q/A)
  Includes index.
  ISBN 978-1-60596-068-5 (hard cover : alk. paper) -- ISBN 978-1-60596-069-2 (soft cover : alk. paper)
  1. Crime scene searches--Juvenile literature. 2. Forensic sciences--Juvenile literature. 3. Criminal investigation--Juvenile literature. I. Title.
  HV8073.8.P367 2009
  363.25--dc22
                        2009005627

Printed in China
1 2 3 4 5 6 7 8 9 0 13 12 11 10 09

Project Coordinator
Heather C. Hudak

Design
Terry Paulhus

Photo credits
Weigl acknowledges Getty Images as its primary image supplier for this title.

CONTENTS

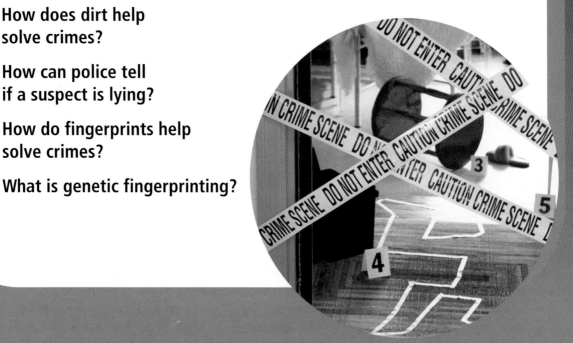

What is crime?

Any action that is against the law can be termed a crime. Every society in the world has crime. Wherever there are people, there are crimes committed. Science plays an important role in crime. With the help of science, we can prevent many crimes from happening, as well as solve crimes already committed. If a crime occurs, science helps us to investigate it. Science also helps us understand how the crime took place, catch criminal suspects, and make sure that a court jury is convinced of the suspect's guilt by providing scientific **evidence** of his or her wrongdoing.

What is a crime scene?

The first step in investigating a crime is usually responding to a telephone call. Police immediately go to the crime scene.

find it quick

Learn how crime scene investigation works at **science.howstuffworks.com/csi.htm**.

A crime scene is the location where a crime has taken place. Examples of crime scenes can be buildings that have been broken into or the place where an injured or dead person has been found. If the scene for a murder is a home, the crime scene includes the room where the body was found, as well as the rest of the house. Police search the entire premises for clues that may help them solve the crime.

Crime scenes are blocked off so that the evidence is not disturbed. Even the most careful criminals usually leave clues behind. Before the evidence is collected, police take photographs of the area. They then collect anything that could be a clue to the crime. Police wear plastic gloves whenever they collect a piece of evidence so that they do not leave their own fingerprints on the object. They place all evidence in separate plastic bags that are then labeled as per contents. Investigators change their gloves often so that they do not move tiny bits from one piece of evidence to another. After all the evidence has been collected, it is taken to a police laboratory for analysis. Police use this evidence to answer questions about the crime. These activities are categorized as a special task called crime scene investigation.

■ According the to U.S. Department of Justice, this is a breakdown of how often different types of crimes occur in the United States.

Ever 22.4 seconds	One Violent Crime
Every 31.0 minutes	One Murder
Every 1.2 minutes	One Robbery
Every 36.8 second	Aggravated Assault
Every 3.2 seconds	**One Property Crime**
Every 14.5 seconds	One Burglary
Every 4.8 seconds	One Larceny-theft
Every 28.8 seconds	One Motor Vehicle Theft

Find the Evidence

The evidence used to resolve an issue can be split into two areas, testimonial evidence and physical evidence. Testimonial evidence is any witnessed account of an incident. Physical evidence refers to any material items that would be present on the crime scene.

How do police know which gun was used in a crime?

If police find a weapon near a crime scene, they need to find out whether it was used to commit the crime.

find it quick

Use your knowledge of guns and help solve crimes while playing fun games at **www.fbi.gov/fbikids.htm**.

Police look at the bullets found in the victim's body or at the crime scene. The study of guns and bullets in criminal investigations is called **ballistics**. Unused bullets are smooth on the outside. When fired from a gun, the bullet gets scratched as it moves through the barrel of the gun. Unique lines and ridges are left on the bullet. Bullets fired from the same gun have the same unique ridges.

If police find a gun they think may have been used in a crime, they will test fire some bullets from that gun. If the ridges on the bullets they fire match those on the bullet found at the crime scene, police confirm that the gun was used for the crime.

To determine whether two bullets were fired from the same gun, police examine the bullets, looking for scratches made by the barrel of the gun. If both bullets have the same scratches, police know they were fired from the same gun.

■ A specialist observes the scratches on a bullet to determine which gun it was fired from.

How do scientists know the cause of death?

An autopsy is the detailed study of the body of the victim. An autopsy is often performed when someone dies, especially if the death occurs in suspicious circumstances.

find it quick

For more information on autopsies, visit **www.pathguy.com/autopsy.htm**.

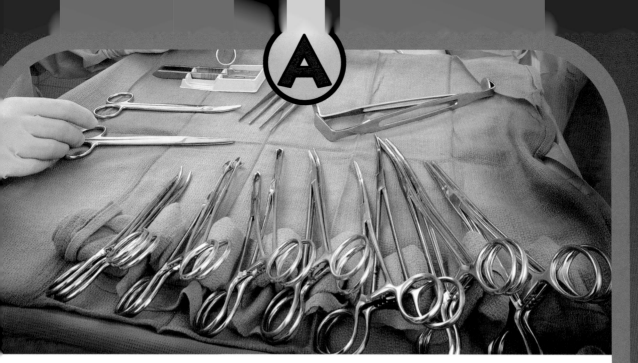

Ⓐ

■ Surgical tools are used to perform autopsies.

Usually an autopsy can help tell how and when a person died. Autopsies are done by forensic pathologists in a medical laboratory. To do an autopsy, a pathologist first looks closely at the body of the dead person. Bruises, wounds, or marks of any kind are photographed and described in writing. If there are gunshot wounds, the pathologist can help determine what type of gun was used and how close the gun was to the victim when it was fired. Any pieces of bullet found are removed.

If there are knife wounds, the pathologist counts the wounds and can even determine whether the killer is right-handed or left-handed through the place of wound. Bruise marks around the neck usually mean that the victim was strangled. The bruises are sometimes measured to determine the size of the hands of the killer.

After examining the outside of the body, the pathologist cuts the body open. The organs are removed and weighed. Any food in the stomach is examined. At this point, scientists also check the presence of any poisons by testing body fluids.

The Inside Story

The Egyptians were one of the first civilizations to practice the removal and examination of the internal organs of humans.

How do scientists determine the time of death?

When investigating a murder case, pathologists must try to figure out exactly when the victim died. This information helps narrow down suspects. To estimate the time of death, pathologists look for various pointers.

find it quick

Learn more about the role of insects at a crime scene at **www.aabaca.com/csi.html**.

After death, body temperature steadily cools down until it is the same as the temperature of the surrounding area. By understanding how fast a body cools down under different conditions, scientists can roughly estimate the time of death. Another factor police use to find the time of death is lividity. This refers to the color of areas on a dead body that darken after death. Gravity causes blood in a victim's body to settle in the areas that are closest to the ground. Lividity usually occurs half an hour to 3 hours after a person's death. Scientists can tell that a body was moved after that time if the dark marks are not close to the ground.

About 3 to 5 hours after death, the muscles in a body usually become stiff. This condition is known as **rigor mortis**. Rigor mortis disappears about 24 to 36 hours after death. If rigor mortis is present in a victim, scientists know that the death happened in the previous day and a half.

Decomposition is the breakdown of cells in a plant or animal that is no longer alive. This begins immediately after death. Scientists are often able to estimate the time of death by looking at how much decomposition has taken place. Decomposition is caused by

■ The female blue bottle fly lays her eggs in the dead animal. The eggs hatch into maggots that immediately begin to eat the dead flesh, causing it to decompose.

bacteria and fungi that cannot survive on a living organism. They cause the body to change color and produce odors.

Insects cause decomposition by laying eggs on the body. When the eggs hatch, the larvae feed on the skin and tissues. Various insects lay their eggs at different times. Some insects lay their eggs soon after a person has died. Others will not lay their eggs until a body has been dead for months.

In addition, all insects have life cycles. Many insects, for example, begin their lives as eggs, hatch into larvae, and then change into their adult form. By determining the insects' stage of life, scientists can estimate how long a person has been dead.

How do investigators identify forgeries and counterfeits?

Forgeries, or fakes, are copies of an object. These are made to trick people into believing that an item is genuine.

find it
quick

Spot the counterfeit painting at
**www.gamesforthebrain.com/
game/counterfeit.**

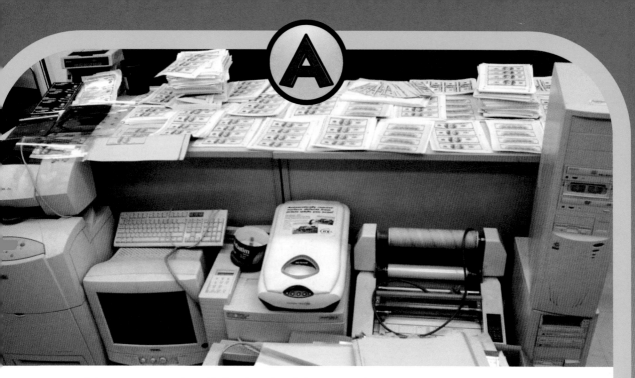

■ Counterfeit currency copies all the details of the original currency.

Criminals are known to make copies of famous paintings, jewelry, and important documents, such as wills. Criminals sometimes also forge a signature on a check or credit card receipt in order to steal money or merchandise.

Scientists use many different methods to find out if something is genuine or a forgery. Most artists have a way of painting or drawing that makes their work unique and difficult to copy. Paints and other materials that are used today are different from those used many years ago. By analyzing the chemicals in a painting, scientists can often tell whether or not the painting is real.

People also make fake money, called counterfeit money. New technologies, such as color **laser** printers make it easier for criminals to make counterfeit notes. Most countries add details to their currency, which makes it very difficult to copy.

Investigators look for these special features when they are trying to find out if money is genuine or counterfeit. For instance, some bills now have small **holograms**, which cannot be copied easily. Most bills also have words written on them in very small letters. These tiny words are very difficult to copy. Another way to identify counterfeit money is to test the paper and ink. Counterfeiters cannot easily get the same materials that are used to make money.

What can scientists tell from a piece of writing?

Every person's handwriting is unique. Police analyze handwriting to learn more about a crime. The study of handwriting is called graphology.

find it quick

Visit **http://science.howstuffworks.com/ handwriting-analysis.htm/printable**, and learn more about graphology in forensics.

Even though handwriting can change depending on a person's mood or how quickly a person writes, certain details about the writing stay the same.

Handwriting experts, or graphologists, are trained to spot differences between people's handwriting. By comparing several different pieces of writing, they can often decide who wrote a ransom letter or forged a name on a check.

People with certain mental illnesses may be more likely to commit a crime and sometimes have a specific type of handwriting. If someone is receiving threatening letters from an unknown person, a graphologist can look at the writing and help determine if the person writing the letters is dangerous.

A graphologist may also be able to look at a letter and know whether the writer was lying or telling the truth.

■ The study of handwriting is called graphology. A person's handwriting offers information about their personality and behavior.

"Write" Styles

The writing characteristics we learn in school, our style characteristics, become the underlying method of our handwriting. We later develop individual characteristics that are unique to us and distinguish our handwriting from someone else's.

17

How do cloth fibers help police investigate crimes?

As people move, tiny fibers fall from their clothing. These fibers float in the air and attach themselves to other objects or people. If you sit in a car, for example, you are likely to pick up fibers from the material on the seats or the floor. These tiny fibers can help link a suspect to a crime.

find it quick

Learn more about **forensic science** at **www.all-about-forensic-science.com/ science-for-kids.html**.

■ Computers can analyze fibers with great precision.

Fibers are usually difficult to see without help from a magnifying glass or a powerful microscope. Police officers often use tape to collect fibers from a crime scene or a suspect's clothes. The fibers are taken to a police lab and examined under a microscope. Fibers that look similar to the human eye look very different under a microscope. Microscopes make it easy to tell wool, cotton, nylon, polyester, and other types of fibers from one another. Bumps and ridges often show up on the strands. If fibers found in two different places look the same, they are analyzed chemically to tell whether they may have come from the same source.

Some types of fibers are common, such as those found in blue jeans. These fibers may not be useful to police because they are found nearly everywhere. Other fibers, however, are very rare. They may have been made years ago or made only in one country. They may be colored by a dye that is not very common. Police try to trace manufacturers to find out who bought products made with these fibers.

Here is your challenge!

Use pieces of tape to remove a single fiber from several cloth items. Tape the fibers to a piece of white paper. Examine each fiber with a magnifying glass. They will differ in color, thickness, and shape. Can you tell which item each fiber came from?

How do police use photography to investigate crimes?

At a crime scene, a police photographer takes many photographs to use as evidence.

find it quick

Learn more about how crimes are investigated at **http://whyfiles.org/014forensic**.

The photographer takes photos of the entire crime scene and close-up photos of any victims. Other types of evidence, including blood stains, footprints, and tire tracks are also photographed. These photographs later help remind investigators about some of the details they may have forgotten. Photographs may also be used in court to help prove the guilt or innocence of a suspect.

Police photographers also take photos of anyone who has been arrested. These photographs are called mug shots. If a criminal escapes from jail, police sometimes publish mug shots in the newspaper or show them on television. They do this in the hope that someone reading the paper or watching television will recognize the person and come forward to give information that may help police find the criminal.

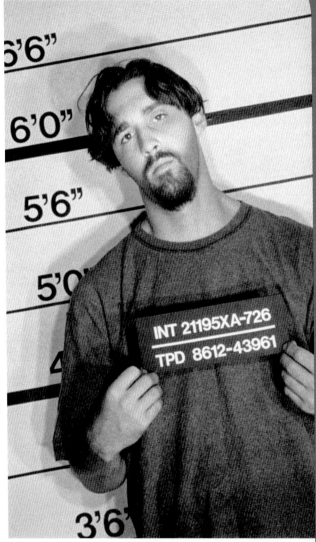

■ Suspects are photographed with names and identification numbers.

Snap Snippet

Even evidence that can only be seen under a microscope can be photographed. These pictures are called photomicrographs.

How does dirt help solve crimes?

Plants and dirt can help investigators link a suspect to a crime scene.

find it quick

Learn more about forensic botany at
www.botany.org/PlantTalkingPoints/crime.php.

■ Mud tracks made by tires show the direction a vehicle was moving.

Although most dirt looks the same, if examined under a microscope, dirt from different areas contains different things. If dirt found on a suspect's shoes or car tires matches the dirt found at the crime scene, police try to prove that the suspect was at the crime scene. Dirt is also useful for showing footprints or tire tracks.

If footprints are found at a crime scene, investigators photograph the prints and make a plaster cast of them. At the police laboratory, scientists can determine that the prints came from a certain make and size of shoe. They can estimate how much the person weighs by how deep the imprints are in the ground. The design and depth of car tire tracks can sometimes help police figure out the type of car that was used by a suspect.

Plants also help investigators. Pollen, for instance, shows where a person has been. Pollen is found in most flowering plants. As people walk past plants, pollen sticks to their clothing or shoes. Different places have different types of pollen. If there is pollen on the clothing of a victim or suspect, or if pollen is found at the crime scene, police may be able to use that information to help solve the crime.

Here is your challenge!

Ride your bike through soft sand, and examine the tire tread pattern that is left behind. How does the pattern change if the tires are not fully inflated?

How can police tell if a suspect is lying?

Scientists invented a lie detector machine that keeps track of the internal body changes that occur when someone is lying. Lie detectors, also called polygraph machines, usually help police decide whether or not someone is telling the truth.

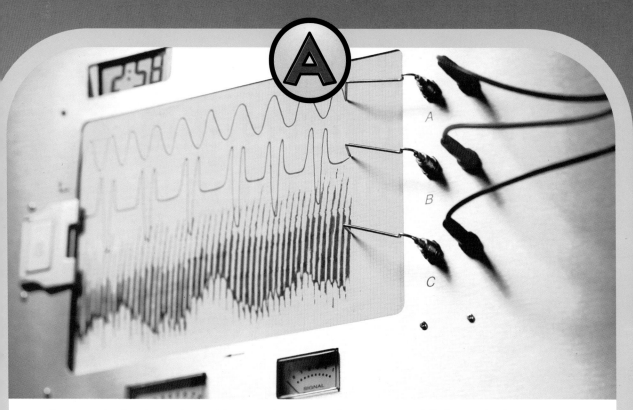

Computerized polygraph machines track a suspect's responses while he or she is being questioned.

Most of us have been raised to believe that it is wrong to lie. We usually feel guilty when we do not tell the truth. When we lie, our body language often gives us away. We turn our eyes away and start to fidget. Many things also happen inside our bodies when we lie. For example, we may start to perspire, and our hearts may beat faster.

A polygraph machine measures breathing rate, pulse rate, blood pressure, and sweat production. To analyse a person as he talks, a person is connected to the polygraph and asked several questions. If the person lies when answering some of the questions, the machine measures changes in the pulse rate and other body functions.

Although polygraphs are useful to police, they are not perfect. Some people are able to lie without any physical changes. Other people are so nervous of being questioned that they experience many physical changes even when they are telling the truth. The test could show that they are lying when they are not. Some countries allow the results of lie detectors to be used against suspected criminals in court. Others do not believe that the results from polygraphs can always be trusted and do not allow such test results to be used as evidence.

How do fingerprints help solve crimes?

No two people in the world have the same fingerprints. Even identical twins who may be exactly alike have different fingerprints.

find it quick

Play an interactive game, and solve a murder mystery at **www.mysterynet.com**.

Fingerprints are one of the most important tools that investigators have to help them solve crimes. The use of fingerprints to solve crimes began in the 1880s. A British scientist named Sir Francis Galton developed a method to help police use fingerprints to identify criminals.

There are natural oils on our skin that rub off on everything we touch. Every time we touch something with our hands, we leave an image of our fingerprints on it. Most of the time, fingerprints that are left on objects are invisible. Scientists have learned how to make the prints visible and collect samples that they can analyze.

The first method is to dust any areas that may have fingerprints. Usually, a fine dusting powder containing aluminum is used. Aluminum is a metal that reflects light, so it makes the fingerprints easier to see and to photograph. Aluminum dusting powder also shows up against both light and dark backgrounds. After dusting, fingerprints are collected in two ways. They are photographed with a zoom lens on a camera, or lifted off the surface. To lift fingerprints, police place a piece of transparent tape on the dusted print. When the tape is carefully peeled off, the image of the fingerprint in the dust is transferred to the tape. The tape of the fingerprint is then placed on a piece of paper or cardboard. It is then either photographed or taken back to the police laboratory.

The second method police use to find fingerprints is to illuminate surfaces with a laser. A laser is a powerful beam of light. When the laser lights up an area, certain substances in fingerprints make them glow. Lasers work well to help find fingerprints that are spread out over a large area. Often, a laser will show fingerprints in a place where a police officer may not have thought to look.

■ Sir Francis Galton was one of the first people to use fingerprinting techniques scientifically.

What is genetic fingerprinting?

Genetic fingerprinting is not just used to find criminals. It is also used to identify dead bodies and even to prove that someone is innocent.

find it quick

Learn more about genetics at **www.kidsturncentral.com/ links/geneticslinks.htm**.

A

Fingerprints are transferred onto film, where they are enlarged and studied.

Some criminals wear gloves while they commit a crime so that they will not leave fingerprints behind. Most of the time, however, criminals leave behind some trace of themselves in the form of hair, blood, or saliva. A thief breaking into a building, for example, may leave a drop of blood after breaking a window to enter. Tiny clues like these can help police find a criminal.

DNA, or deoxyribonucleic acid, is found in most cells of every living organism. DNA contains all of the information that makes one living thing different from another. The color of our eyes and hair, for example, is coded within our own DNA. Except for identical twins, every person in the world has different DNA.

Police take all samples of blood, hair, and other bodily traces from the crime scene. Not all samples contain DNA. Hair, for example, does not contain DNA unless the piece of hair has a root from the scalp on the end. Once cell samples that contain DNA have been found, forensic scientists test them using a special technique. The results of this test give a "picture" or "fingerprint" of a person's DNA. If the genetic fingerprint found in the evidence matches that of a suspect, the chances are good that police have found the right person.

How do police identify a victim from bones or teeth?

Sometimes, the police have only bones left from a victim of crime. If the teeth are present, they may be compared with dental records to help identify the person. Otherwise, a **forensic anthropologist** studies the bones to find out information about the victim.

The Kingdoms of Life

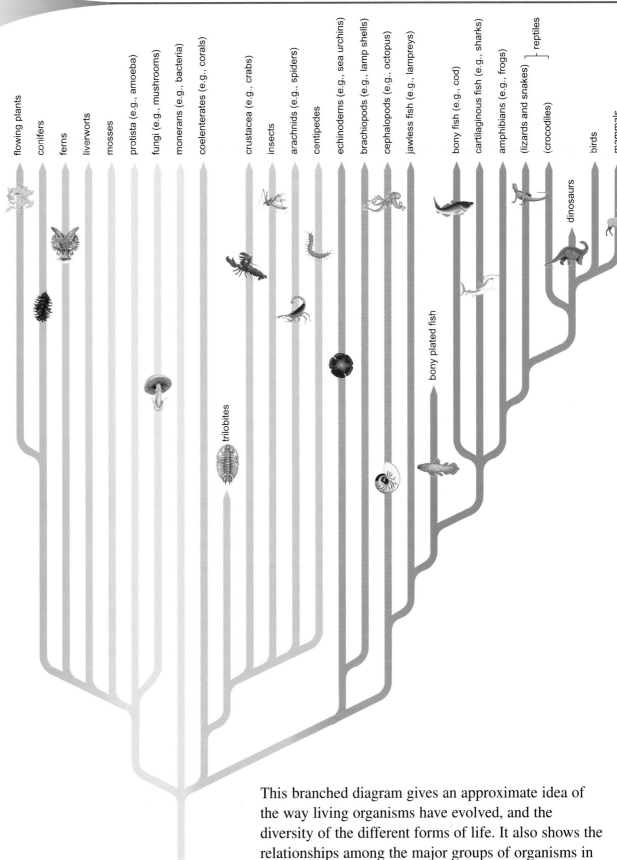

flowing plants
conifers
ferns
liverworts
mosses
protista (e.g., amoeba)
fungi (e.g., mushrooms)
monerans (e.g., bacteria)
coelenterates (e.g., corals)
crustacea (e.g., crabs)
insects
arachnids (e.g., spiders)
centipedes
echinoderns (e.g., sea urchins)
brachiopods (e.g., lamp shells)
cephalopods (e.g., octopus)
jawless fish (e.g., lampreys)
bony fish (e.g., cod)
cartilaginous fish (e.g., sharks)
amphibians (e.g., frogs)
(lizards and snakes)
reptiles
(crocodiles)
birds
mammals
dinosaurs
bony plated fish
trilobites

This branched diagram gives an approximate idea of the way living organisms have evolved, and the diversity of the different forms of life. It also shows the relationships among the major groups of organisms in the five **kingdom** system of classification.

44   monerans

A modern catastrophe

Extinctions that result from human activity have several different causes and some are more obvious than others. Some species have been hunted to extinction. The passenger pigeon existed in huge numbers in eastern North America. However, early settlers killed so many of these birds that by the end of the nineteenth century the population had declined from billions of birds to zero. Less well known is the fact that two species of lice that were dependent on the bird became extinct, too.

A more important cause of extinctions today is the loss of habitat. Habitat destruction worldwide is taking place at a tremendous rate. The losses are greatest in tropical rain forests, where the diversity of species is also highest. More than half of these rain forests have already been cut down for timber and farming.

Another human cause of extinctions has been the introduction of non-native species into habitats. Many extinctions have taken place on islands, where species with no natural enemies are particularly at risk from the introduction of predators such as cats and rats that are brought in either accidentally or deliberately.

The next wave

After every mass extinction that has taken place over the long history of life on Earth, diversity has increased to a greater level than it was at previously. It is sobering to think that no matter what we do, we will not be able to stop life in its tracks. Not even the **asteroid** that shattered the dinosaurs' world could do that. There is greater diversity now than ever before, but it has taken a very long recovery time— 65 million years—for this diversity to evolve.

This region of Costa Rica was once rain forest, but the trees have been clear-cut and now cattle graze here. Clear-cutting of rain forests could cause a mass extinction.

A forensic anthropologist can tell whether bones belong to a man or a woman. Women's bones are smaller than men's bones. Women also have wider pelvic bones than men. If the person ever broke a bone, the healed break will show even after death. Bones give an idea of how tall a person was. Scientists can also guess an age range from bones. Bones of a very old person look different from the bones of a young person.

Forensic anthropologists use plastic or clay to try to make a face on the victim's skull. This is called **facial reconstruction**. Scientists know how thick the skin and muscles are on different parts of the face. By building up these areas on the skull, they create a face that looks much like that of the person when he or she was alive. By adding eyes, teeth, and hair, the forensic anthropologist can create a face that may be recognized and identified.

There are slight differences in the size of teeth of each individual. Dental records, which are kept for anyone who has ever been to a dentist, are useful in identifying people. Teeth are not as useful as fingerprints, because dental records change as a person gets older, but dental records can still help identify victims.

■ Forensic pathologists compare DNA samples collected from corpses with samples taken from family members of the deceased.

Here is your challenge!

Collect a strand of hair from four different people. Look at the hair under a magnifying glass. Note the texture and color differences in each strand of hair. Can you tell who each hair belongs to?

How do artists help police investigations?

Witnesses to a crime have seen the suspect, and they know what he or she looks like. When this happens, the witness describes the suspect to a police artist.

■ Based on the artist's drawing, suspects are lined up for identification by witnesses.

Using the description, the police artist either draws the face on paper, or creates a face with a computer program. The artist emphasizes any of the suspect's unique features, such as a large nose or buckteeth. The resulting picture is called a **composite**. The witness keeps asking that changes be made to the composite until it looks like the suspect.

Once a composite is complete, police show the picture to other potential witnesses or anyone who might recognize the face. Sometimes, composites are printed on posters that describe the crime and ask anyone who recognizes the face to contact the police.

Eye Witness

If you are a witness to a crime and the police have a suspect, they may show you several pictures of people who look similar to the suspect. They also include a photograph of the suspect. If you choose their suspect, it helps to confirm that they are after the right person.

What is a profiler?

Sometimes, police have evidence of a crime, but they may not have any good leads as to who committed the crime. If the crime is a serious one, such as murder, the police ask for help from a psychological profiler.

find it quick

Learn more about psychological profiling at **http://library.thinkquest.org/04oct/00206/ nts_psychological_profiling.htm**.

Profilers are psychologists who study how criminal minds work. A profiler studies all the details of a crime to come up with an idea of what type of person the killer is. The profiler tries to understand why the criminal has committed such a crime. Profilers might determine the gender, age, job, and even habits of the criminal.

The details that the profiler gives to police are compared to descriptions of anyone connected with the crime. If the description fits someone, that person is questioned further.

When police suspect that one person has committed a number of crimes, they sometimes work with a **geographic profiler**. Using information about the location of the crimes, a geographic profiler can determine where the person who committed the crimes most likely lives.

Geographic profiling helps investigators find an offender's most likely location.

Guilty as Charged

Police investigations can lead to a list of thousands of suspects for one crime. In the case of the "Green River Killer" in the United States, police had collected the names of 18,000 suspects. On November 30, 2001, Gary Leon Ridgway, a.k.a. the Green River Killer, was arrested for the murders of four women whose cases were linked to him through DNA evidence.

What are voiceprints?

Each of us has a unique way of speaking. Like our fingerprints, our speech habits are different from those of other people. Even if someone disguises his or her voice, the same speech patterns are present.

A

■ Voiceprints are made from spectrograms. A spectrogram is a graph that shows sound frequency. Different speech sounds create different shapes within the graph. Spectrograms also use colors or shades of gray to represent the qualities of sound.

In certain crimes, police sometimes have a recording of voices as evidence. Obscene telephone calls, bomb threats, and ransom demands are often recorded over the telephone. Scientists listen to different voice recordings to figure out whether they were spoken by the same person.

To compare voices, scientists take two sample recordings and analyze them with a sound spectrograph. This machine creates a voiceprint of each of the taped voices. Voiceprints are graphs made of the voice sounds recorded on tape. Scientists then examine the voiceprints for similarities.

Open Sesame!

Voiceprints are used to protect buildings and computers. A person speaks into the system, and a program compares his or her speech patterns to the voiceprint registered in the system. If the voiceprints match, the person is allowed access to the building or the computer.

What are blood types?

Genetic fingerprinting is useful in helping prove a suspect's guilt or innocence. However, testing DNA takes a great deal of time and can be very expensive. Before doing genetic fingerprinting, police usually check the type of blood that has been found at a crime scene and the blood of the victims and suspects.

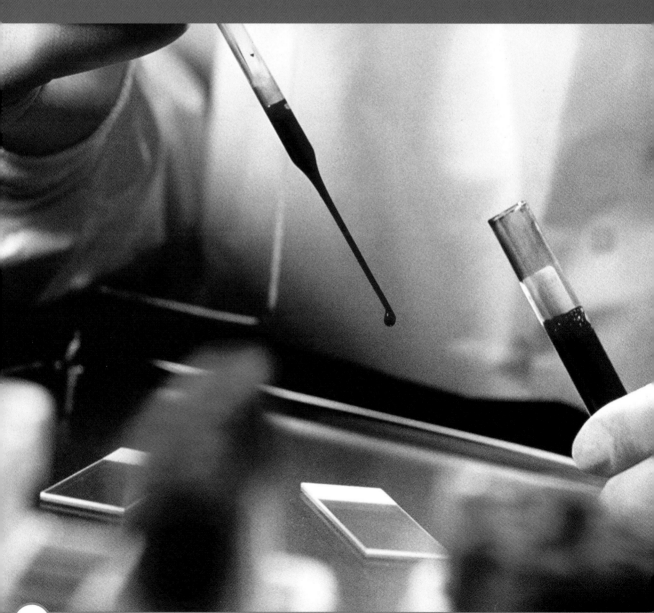

Although blood from different people looks the same, it can be quite different. Scientists can quickly tell if blood is from a human or from an animal. If they find human blood, they look at many different parts of blood cells to determine the blood's group, or type. One way to distinguish between different types of blood is to use the ABO system. In this system, all human blood is divided into four types: A, B, AB, and O. Each person's blood is one of these types.

Millions of people in the world have the same blood types, so the ABO system is not always useful in a criminal investigation. If two people have the same blood type, there are other chemicals in the blood that may help scientists tell from whom the blood sample came.

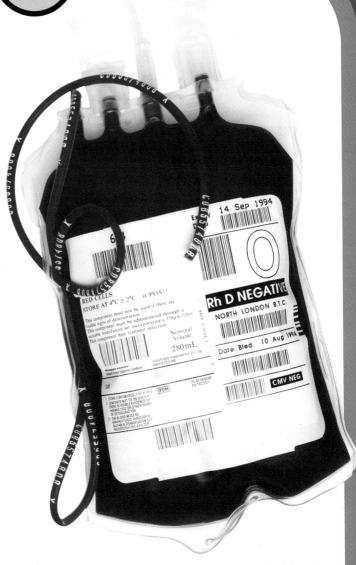

■ Blood type can be studied after the blood is collected and stored in special sealed bags.

"O" Yeah!

In a medical emergency, people may need blood to survive. Mixing blood types can kill the person who receives blood. Type O blood is the only type that can be given to anyone. However, people with type O blood must receive type O blood.

How do burglar alarms work?

Burglar alarms can help prevent thieves from breaking into homes, offices, and other buildings.

A burglar alarm system uses sensors to detect anyone who enters a building through an unauthorized entry. If these sensors detect that someone has forced an entry or is in the building, an alarm is set off.

Burglar alarms often work by emitting loud noises, which are intended to scare away intruders. Some alarm systems are connected to the police or to a security company. These alarms may or may not make a noise. When they go off, the police or security officers are sent to the building to see what has happened. There are two main types of burglar alarms: magnetic and infrared.

Magnetic burglar alarms use sensors placed on each window and door of a building. The sensors are made of two parts held together by sealed magnets. If one of the doors or windows is opened, the two parts of the sensor are pulled apart. A signal is then sent to the alarm system, which sets the alarm off.

Infrared burglar alarms can sense movement within a building. They do this by sensing heat, or infrared radiation, which is given off by all people and animals. We cannot see heat energy, but infrared sensors can detect it. The sensors even work in the dark. If the sensors detect any movement in areas where there should be no people, an alarm is set off.

■ The U.S. Department of Justice lists the place and time burglaries took place in 2007.

Burglary by location	Total*	2007
		2,179,140
Residence (dwelling)		1,478,901
Residence Night		421,855
Residence Day		738,654
Residence Unknown		318,392
Nonresidence (store, office, etc.)		700,239
Nonresidence Night		293,469
Nonresidence Day		227,092
Nonresidence Unknown		179,670

*Because of rounding, the number of burglaries may not add to the total

Here is your challenge!

Make a burglar alarm by filling tin cans or soda cans with small pebbles. Use string to hang the cans across the place you want to keep safe. You can set up a stack of cans or bottles so that, if the door is opened, they fall down and make a noise. The key is to make a noise that alerts others to the intrusion.

How do computers help solve crimes?

Computers are important tools in the fight against crime. Investigators use them to store large amounts of information and to retrieve it quickly and easily.

At one time, all information was recorded on paper and kept in files. Using this storage method meant spending a long time to find one specific file. It is much faster to search for information on a computer. Finding information quickly is important to police investigators. Computers assist police by storing large numbers and different types of records.

Many investigating organizations keep computer databases that contain information about people's DNA and fingerprints. This information is easy for investigators to find and may greatly speed up the investigation. For example, if a fingerprint is found at a crime scene, a computer quickly compares it to the thousands of fingerprints on record. If a match is found, the police may have found their culprit. Before computers, this type of search was done by hand. Police spent hundreds of hours trying to match a fingerprint from a crime scene with the hundreds of fingerprints on record. Computers now do this search in just a few minutes.

Computers help police in other ways as well. Using computers, police can find addresses, owners of vehicles, and even photos of criminals in seconds. Police can quickly receive helpful information from

■ Some police vehicles are fitted with computers so important information can be transferred immediately to them.

other police agencies around the world. Some computer programs can determine what a missing person might look like after several years. If a child disappeared 10 years ago, for instance, a computer program would be able to show what that child might look like now. This can be useful in helping to find the child.

Crime Careers

Law Enforcement Officers

If you like the idea of preventing crime and protecting people, you might want to become a law enforcement officer. Police officer or detective are just two of the many different jobs in law enforcement.

The police officer's most important tasks are to protect people and catch criminals. Some patrol certain areas on foot or in their vehicles to make sure that no crimes are being committed. They also respond to emergency helpline calls.

Detectives catch people who commit crimes and identify victims. They are also called criminal investigators because they investigate, or find information about, crimes. They look for evidence, interview witnesses and suspects, and make arrests if necessary.

Forensic Scientists

Forensic science helps investigators find and analyze evidence that can be used in a court of law. Forensic scientists use technology to examine physical evidence found during criminal investigations. They usually work in police laboratories and play an important part in solving crimes. There are many different types of forensic scientists, each specializing in a particular subject.

Forensic pathologists are doctors who examine bodies to find out how and when death occurred. Forensic anthropologists specialize in studying bones found at crime scenes. Forensic biologists study body fluids, such as blood or saliva, that have been left at a crime scene. DNA specialists are experts in studying DNA. Forensic entomologists study insects found at a crime scene.

find it
quick

Learn more about careers in crime at
http://www.sfccmo.edu/pages/585.asp.

Young scientists at work

Fact

No two people in the world have the same fingerprints. This makes fingerprinting a valuable tool for law enforcement officers when trying to identify a suspect.

Test

See how well your crime detection abilities work with this activity.

Looking for Fingerprints

Materials

Ink pad, white paper, dusting powder (cocoa or chocolate powder), paintbrush, glass, tape

1. Ask your family members or friends to let you fingerprint them. Press each finger firmly on the ink pad and then on the piece of paper. Label each print with the name of the person and the finger it came from.

2. Find a smooth object, such as a mirror or a glass, that one of your family members has recently touched. With the paintbrush, gently brush some dusting powder onto the object.

3. If you uncover a fingerprint, press a piece of clear tape gently but firmly over the print.

4. Carefully remove the tape, and place it on the white paper.

5. Compare the print to the ones you collected earlier. Can you figure out which person (and which finger) the print belongs to? See if you can find fingerprints on other items around your home.

Take a science survey

Examine your house outside and inside to see how safe it is.

1. Compare your home to others on your street. If you were a criminal, is there some reason why your home would be more appealing than another? Burglars often look for homes that have hiding spots, such as trees or bushes near doors or windows. This means that they have a better chance of breaking into a home without being seen. If your home looks more expensive than others around it, a burglar might assume that there are more objects of value inside.

2. Examine the locks on your doors and windows. Do your doors have locks only on the handles, or do they also have stronger deadbolt locks? Do all of your windows lock? Are any windows easy to get to by climbing on something nearby? Many burglars enter homes through unlocked doors and windows. Do you keep your doors and windows locked?

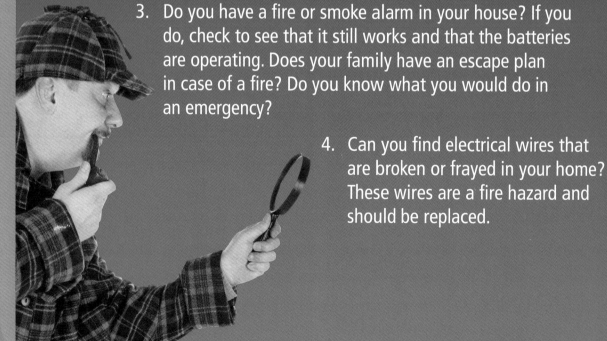

3. Do you have a fire or smoke alarm in your house? If you do, check to see that it still works and that the batteries are operating. Does your family have an escape plan in case of a fire? Do you know what you would do in an emergency?

4. Can you find electrical wires that are broken or frayed in your home? These wires are a fire hazard and should be replaced.

Fast Facts

If all the DNA in a human cell were stretched out, it would be more than 6 feet (2 meters) long.

The insects most often found on dead bodies are the larvae of the common blue bottle fly, the greenbottle fly, and the housefly.

Police dogs are trained to attack criminals on command, follow scents, and sniff out drugs or weapons in luggage at airports.

In the United States, the FBI has a list of the "top 10 most wanted" criminals in America. The FBI posts photographs of the criminals on its website and sends copies to other law enforcement agencies around the world.

At the scene of a hit-and-run car accident, police collect any chips of paint left by the car that fled. They analyze the paint to find out what type of car they should look for.

Some copier machines are designed to recognize money from many countries. If someone tries to copy money on one of these machines, the copies will come out as blank pieces of paper.

Before fingerprinting was used, police identified people using "man measurement." They believed that it was rare for two people to have the exact same body measurements.

Police investigating a crime will usually go through garbage at the crime scene and at a suspect's home and workplace, looking for clues.

Since tattoos are permanent, they help the police identify criminals and victims.

Some murders are made to look like suicides. Pathologists can often tell whether or not someone committed suicide by determining the angle of the wound made by a bullet or a knife.

Glossary

ballistics: the study of firearms and bullets

composite: a sketch or image of a person made by a police artist based on a description from a witness

DNA: the genetic chemical in cells that directs all function and development

evidence: any clues or details that may help investigators solve a crime

facial reconstruction: a method of creating a face by molding clay over the top of a skull

forensic anthropologist: a person who studies bones for information about a person

forensic science: any science that is related to law and can be used as evidence in court

geographic profiler: a person who uses information from crime scenes to determine where a criminal most likely lives

holograms: three-dimensional images produced by lasers

laser: a strong beam of light

rigor mortis: a temporary stiffness of the body that sets into the muscles after death

Index